{ Cape Penguin }

{ Common Frog }

Bone Collection
ANIMALS

{ Green Turtle }

{ Platypus }

ISBN 978-0-545-57628-4

10 9 8 7 6 5 4 3 2 1   13 14 15 16 17

Produced for Marshall Editions by Tall Tree Ltd.
Written by: Rob Colson
Illustrated by: Sandra Doyle, Elizabeth Gray, and Steve Kirk
Designed by: Marisa Renzullo
Consultant: Camilla de la Bédoyère

Printed and bound in China
First Scholastic edition, September 2013

PICTURE CREDITS

Bone *Collection*
ANIMALS

CONTENTS

INTRODUCTION 5

ANIMALS WITH
BACKBONES 6-7

ATLANTIC COD 8-9

FISH 10-11

COMMON FROG 12-13

AMPHIBIANS 14-15

GREEN TURTLE 16-17

TURTLES 18-19

NILE CROCODILE 20-21

CROCODILIANS 22-23

PIT VIPER 24-25

SNAKES 26-27

SCARLET MACAW 28-29

FLYING BIRDS 30-31

CAPE PENGUIN 32-33

FLIGHTLESS BIRDS 34-35

PLATYPUS 36-37

MONOTREMES 38-39

RED KANGAROO 40-41

MARSUPIALS 42-43

FRUIT BAT 44-45

BATS 46-47

BEAVER 48-49

RODENTS 50-51

LION 52-53

CATS 54-55

ELEPHANT SEAL 56-57

SEALS 58-59

BLUE WHALE 60-61

WHALES AND
DOLPHINS 62-63

AFRICAN ELEPHANT .. 64-65

ELEPHANTS 66-67

MOOSE 68-69

DEER AND ANTELOPE .. 70-71

HORSE 72-73

HORSES, ZEBRAS,
AND DONKEYS 74-75

THREE-TOED SLOTH 76-77

TREE MAMMALS 78-79

GIANT ANTEATER 80-81

ANTEATERS 82-83

GORILLA 84-85

APES 86-87

HUMANS 88-89

AMAZING SKELETON
FACTS 90-91

BONE NAMES 92-93

GLOSSARY 94-95

INDEX 96

INTRODUCTION

OUR bony skeletons support and protect our bodies. Without our bones, we would collapse into jelly on the floor! Our skeletons have joints and are attached to muscles, and this allows us to move around. Lots of other animals have skeletons like ours. In this book, we get under the skin of some of them.

{ Fig 1: Indian palm squirrel }

{ Fig 2: Toucan }

We will show you a drawing of the skeleton of one species of animal. These drawings are based on real skeletons, and you'll see exactly how the bones fit together. We will then take a closer look at similar animals, showing you how they live and explaining how different parts of their bodies work. Finally, we will look at the human skeleton, and you will see just how much we have in common with the animals around us!

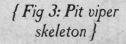

{ Fig 3: Pit viper skeleton }

ANIMALS WITH BACKBONES

THE animals featured in this book are all vertebrates. This means that they have a skeleton with a backbone. Vertebrates come in many different shapes and sizes, but under the skin, they have surprisingly similar skeletons. The backbone extends from the head, where the brain is protected by a skull. Nerves run along the backbone carrying signals between the brain and the body. Compare the different skeletons to one another, and you will see that the bodies of many animals have the same parts, with rib cages to protect important organs such as the heart and lungs, and with arms, legs, flippers, or wings extending from the central body.

Shoulder

Elbow

Radius and ulna

Early Mammals

Bats and seals belong to a group of animals called placental mammals. All placental mammals have a common ancestor that looked like a shrew and lived around 80 million years ago, when dinosaurs still walked the earth.

FIRST VERTEBRATE

The first vertebrate was a small fishlike creature that lived more than 500 million years ago. It was similar to the lamprey, which is still found in rivers and oceans today. Like the lamprey, the first vertebrate did not have jaws. Instead, it had a funnel-like mouth, which it used to suck food into its stomach.

{ Fig 1: Sea lamprey }

COMPARING BONES

Here, we've put the bones of the wing of a fruit bat, the flipper of an elephant seal, and the arm of a human next to one another. Can you tell which is which? The bat's wing is used to fly, the seal's flipper to swim, and a human's arm to pick things up. They all look very different from the outside, but the bones underneath the skin are arranged in the same way. All three have shoulder blades, upper arm and lower arm bones, and "hands" with five "fingers."

"Finger" bones

Shoulder

Humerus

"Hand" bones

ATLANTIC COD

A LARGE fish that lives in the North Atlantic Ocean, the Atlantic cod is a powerful predator. It has a sensitive whisker, called a barbel, on its chin, which it uses to find prey on the seabed.

DORSAL FINS
Each fin contains lots of small bones called fin rays.

Eye socket

Pectoral fins

FIERCE HUNTER
Cod hunt shrimp, crab, and small fish such as herring.

Pelvic fins

FIN CONTROL

The fish pushes itself forward with its dorsal, anal, and tail fins. It uses its pectoral and pelvic fins to change direction.

Fishing Industry

Every year, nearly a million tons of cod are caught by fishermen. Their numbers have fallen sharply, and this has led to calls for a reduction in fishing.

Tail fin

Vertebrae

Anal fins

A fully grown Atlantic cod weighs up to 50 pounds and is more than 3 feet long.

COLD WATERS

Atlantic cod live in cold, shallow water around the coasts of North America and northern Europe. They swim together in large shoals, and feed at mid-depths or near the seafloor.

9

FISH

FISH have been around for 500 million years. They were the earliest animals to have a backbone. Fish breathe using gills, which take oxygen from the water.

LARVAE

Fish lay large numbers of small eggs. The eggs hatch into young called larvae. Many fish feed on larvae and most will be eaten, but some survive to grow into adults.

Sailfish

BOTTOM FEEDER
The plaice fish lies on its side, hiding on the seabed. Both of its eyes are on the same side of its head, so it can still see.

FASTEST FISH
The sailfish is the fastest fish. It can swim at a speed of 68 mph.

Long pectoral fin ↠

SAIL FIN
When it feels threatened, the sailfish raises up its sail-like dorsal fin to make itself look big and scary.

Bendy Body

The skeletons of sharks are not made of bone. Instead, they are made of bendy cartilage—the material your nose is made from. This makes them very flexible.

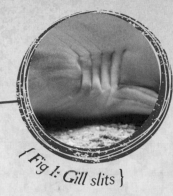

{ Fig 1: Gill slits }

Sharks have between five and seven gill slits on each side of the head.

Spearlike bill

Skin changes color when the fish is excited.

SAFETY IN NUMBERS

Many smaller fish swim in large shoals. This makes it harder for predators to catch them.

DEEP-SEA MONSTER

The viperfish spends its days in the deep oceans where it is totally dark. The fish makes its own light from special organs on the side of its body. Other fish are attracted to the light, and the viperfish snatches them in its large jaws when they draw near.

COMMON FROG

Large skull

THE common frog is an amphibian, which means that it can live on land and in water. It has lungs to breathe air, but it can also take in oxygen through its skin, which allows it to survive long periods underwater.

INSECT HUNTER
The common frog hunts insects, spiders, slugs, and snails. It catches its prey with its long, sticky tongue.

Front feet

The front legs are much smaller than the back legs.

BACKBONE

Frogs have very short spines. This keeps their backs rigid when they jump.

Long Jumper

With their muscular back legs, common frogs can leap up to seven times their own body length. That's the equivalent of a human jumping 13 yards from a stationary position!

HIP BONES

Long hip bones drive a frog's powerful jumps.

This frog is about 4 inches long. It is small enough to sit on the palm of your hand.

Thigh bone

WINTER SLEEP

The common frog spends most of its time on land, hunting in woodlands and fields. But it never strays far from water. Every winter, it finds a damp place under a stone or in a shallow pond, where it hibernates.

The long back feet have webbed toes, which help the frog to swim.

AMPHIBIANS

FROGS, newts, and salamanders are amphibians. Most amphibians spend some time out of the water, but they must keep their skin moist, as this helps them breathe.

CROAKING FROGS

Male frogs croak, or call, to attract females. The females prefer males with loud, deep calls. The males make their calls louder and deeper by inflating special vocal sacs under their mouths.

NEWTS

Newts have lizard-shaped bodies and short legs. They swim using their long, flattened tails.

Vocal sac

Feet

14

TADPOLES

When they hatch, frog larvae are known as tadpoles. They feed and grow in the water, and within a few weeks, they turn into tiny froglets. The froglets grow into full-size adults over the next one to two years.

{ Fig 2: Froglet }

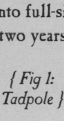

{ Fig 1: Tadpole }

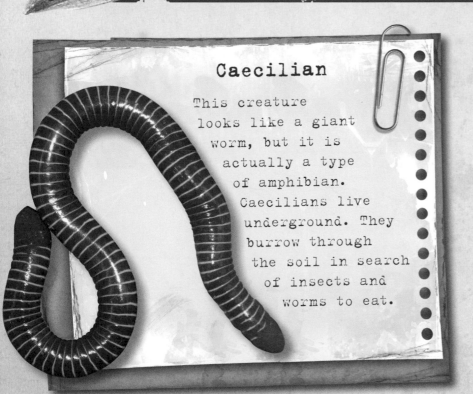

Caecilian

This creature looks like a giant worm, but it is actually a type of amphibian. Caecilians live underground. They burrow through the soil in search of insects and worms to eat.

GIANT SALAMANDER

This is the biggest of all amphibians, growing up to 6 feet long. It feeds on frogs, fish, and mice.

AXOLOTL
The axolotl spends its entire life in water. It breathes through its featherlike gills.

WATER TO LAND
Most amphibians lay their eggs in water. The eggs hatch into larvae, which look very different from the adults. The larvae stay in the water until they have developed into miniature versions of their parents.

GREEN TURTLE

GREEN sea turtles are large reptiles that live in warm tropical oceans. They cruise through the sea, grazing on lush areas of sea grass and seaweed.

BONY SHELL

The turtle's skeleton is surrounded by a hard shell. The rib cage and backbone are joined to a layer of bone. This layer is covered by plates, or scutes, made from keratin—the hard substance your fingernails are made from.

The bones at the top of the head are fused together to form a protective helmet.

Shoulder and hip bones are inside the rib cage.

Ocean Wanderer

The green turtle pulls itself through the water using its long front flippers. The flippers work like oars, beating in the shape of a figure eight.

The paddlelike flippers contain bones similar to our hands, with five sets of "finger" bones.

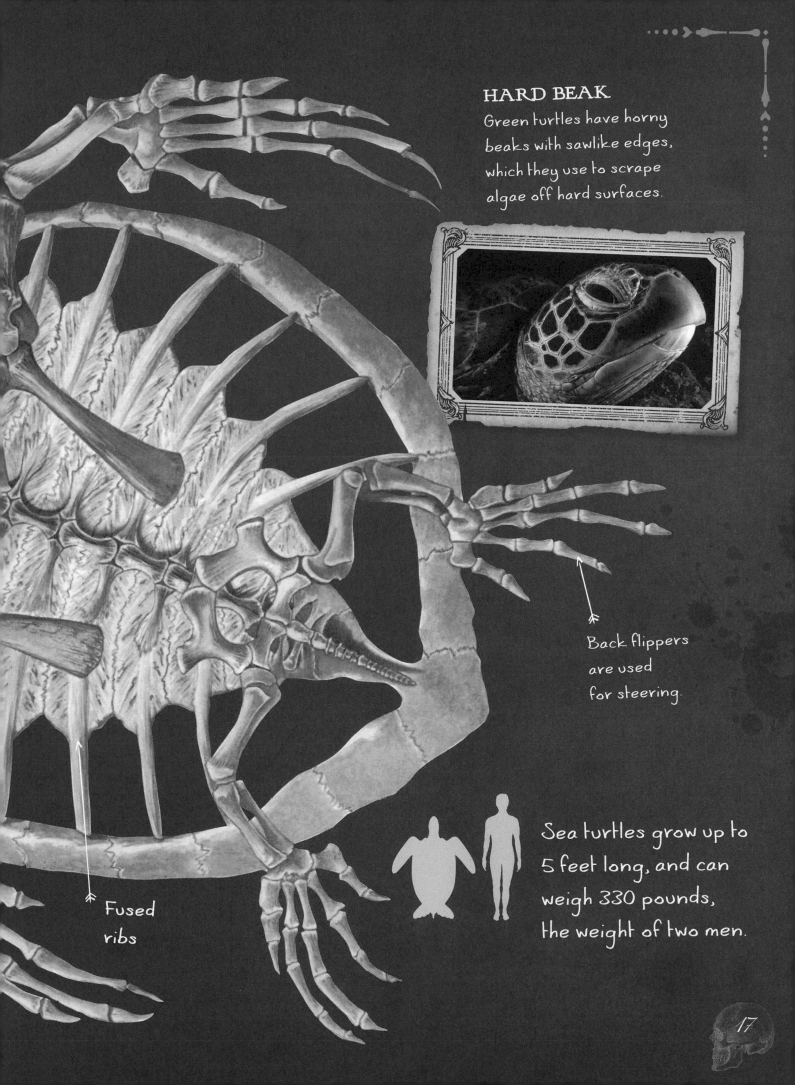

HARD BEAK

Green turtles have horny beaks with sawlike edges, which they use to scrape algae off hard surfaces.

Back flippers are used for steering.

Fused ribs

Sea turtles grow up to 5 feet long, and can weigh 330 pounds, the weight of two men.

TURTLES

TURTLES are protected from predators by built-in armor. When they sense danger, many turtles pull their heads and legs inside their shells, where predators can't get them. Turtles live on land or in water. Those on land are also called tortoises.

LONG LIVES

Turtles can live for a very long time. Giant tortoises have been known to live for more than 200 years!

Giant tortoise

Mouth has a hard beak but no teeth. ➤

Long, flexible neck

HATCHLINGS
The first year of a turtle's life is a very dangerous time. Only one percent of the hatchlings will make it to adulthood.

18

{ Fig 1: Green turtle hatchling }

When they hatch, the young turtles pull themselves out of the sand and make their way to the sea.

Laying Eggs

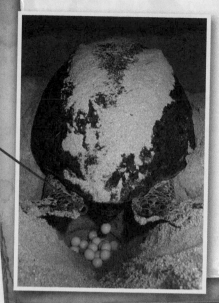

Like most reptiles, turtles lay eggs. Sea turtles lay their eggs on beaches, where they bury the eggs in the sand to keep them safe.

HINGED SHELL

A turtle's shell covers all of its body except the head and legs. The top side is called the carapace, while the bottom side is called the plastron. Some turtles have a hinged plastron, allowing them to pull their heads and legs inside the shell.

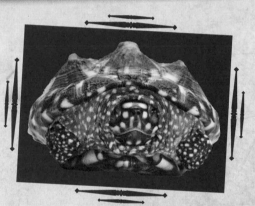

TAKING REFUGE

This young spotted pond turtle has pulled itself right inside its shell.

BREATHING UNDERWATER

Turtles breathe air using lungs, just like us. But some turtles also breathe underwater, like fish. The pig-nosed turtle takes water in through its mouth and passes it out through its large nostrils. A special lining in the mouth absorbs oxygen from the water.

{ Fig 2: Pig-nosed turtle }

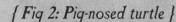

19

NILE CROCODILE

THIS fearsome reptile has been ambushing unsuspecting victims ever since the time of the dinosaurs. The Nile crocodile is at home on land or in the water, and few animals are safe from its attacks.

Strong, flexible backbone

Long jaws are studded with sharp teeth.

Teeth are replaced when they wear out.

KEEP BACK!

You might outsprint a Nile crocodile on land, but in water it can move ten times faster than you. It hides in the water and ambushes large mammals such as antelopes, which come to the waterside to drink.

HIGH WALK

On land, the crocodile moves around mostly by sliding on its belly. But it can run in short bursts by raising itself off the ground in a "high walk," as the skeleton here is doing.

Growing Menace

Crocodiles live for up to 100 years, and they keep growing all their lives. As they grow, their prey changes. The young hunt fish and frogs, while larger adults take on wildebeest and zebras.

Legs raise the body off the ground when running.

MUSCULAR TAIL

Crocodiles swim by swinging their strong, flat tails from side to side.

WEBBED FEET

The four toes on the back foot are webbed. This helps the crocodile steer as it swims.

A mature male Nile crocodile can measure more than 16 feet long and weigh up to one ton.

CROCODILIANS

THE crocodilians are a group of reptiles that includes crocodiles, alligators, and gharials. They are strong swimmers and spend much of their lives in water.

Mouth contains 24 sharp teeth.

POWERFUL BITE

The muscles that close a crocodile's jaws are very powerful. But the muscles that open the mouth are weak—so weak that a human can hold a large crocodile's mouth shut.

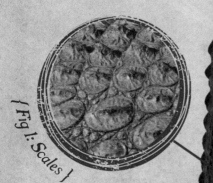

{ Fig 1: Scales }

The skin is protected by a layer of tough, horny scales.

ALLIGATOR

With a wider snout than a crocodile's, an alligator's teeth fit inside its mouth when it's closed.

Keeping Cool

When they fall asleep in the hot sun, crocodiles are in danger of overheating. They stay cool by sleeping with their mouths wide open.

HIDDEN DANGER

The nose and eyes of an alligator are at the top of its head. This allows it to float almost entirely underwater, hidden from its prey.

GHARIAL

The long-snouted gharial lives in rivers and swamps in southern Asia.

FISH EATER

The gharial spends almost all its time in the water, feeding on a diet of fish. It swishes its narrow snout swiftly through the water to catch its fast-moving prey. It then holds on to the slippery meal with its many needlelike teeth.

CARING MOTHER

Just before they hatch, baby crocodiles cry out to their mother from inside their eggs. This is to make sure that the mother is there to guard them when they hatch. The mother then carefully carries the hatchlings in her mouth from the nest down to the water.

{ Fig 2: Crocodile mother }

PIT VIPER

PITS
The small, heat-sensitive pits are found just above the front of the upper jaw.

FANGS
Venom is pumped into the fangs from glands on either side of the head. The venom is injected when the fangs pierce the prey's skin.

THE pit viper lives in the Americas, Europe, and Asia. It hunts in the dark with great accuracy. On each side of its head is a small pit that is sensitive to heat. When an animal comes near, these pits sense its body heat, so the snake knows where to strike!

Backbone

Open Wide

The viper's lightweight skull is made mostly of jaw bones. It can open its mouth very wide because its upper and lower jaws are loosely joined. This allows the snake to swallow large prey whole.

24

NIGHT SENSES

The two heat-sensitive pits, one on either side of the head, produce a stereo effect, allowing the snake to judge distances as well as direction. This allows the snake to strike with accuracy, even in pitch-darkness.

Ribs

The viper grows up to 10 feet in length—that's longer than a man!

Most snakes do not have hip bones, shoulder blades, or leg bones.

The pit viper's skeleton is mostly made up of vertebrae, each with a pair of ribs attached. This snake has about 200 pairs of ribs.

SNAKES

WHEN hunting, snakes use many ways to kill prey and to scare off any predators.

CRAWLING HUNTER

Slithering around on its stomach, a snake can detect the tiniest vibrations in the ground. These could be made by a scuttling mouse, or they could be made by a mongoose that wants to eat the snake!

CRUSHED TO DEATH

Constrictors coil their powerful bodies around prey and then squeeze the life out of them!

UNDER THREAT

When a predator comes near, a rattlesnake rears up and shakes its rattle as a warning.

Scales

Warning Signs

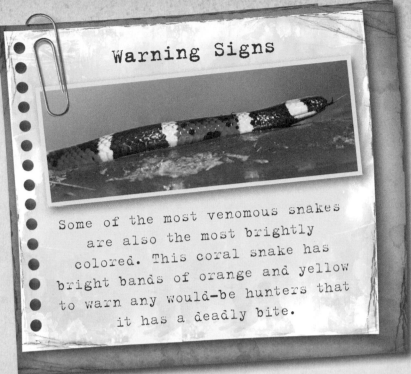

Some of the most venomous snakes are also the most brightly colored. This coral snake has bright bands of orange and yellow to warn any would-be hunters that it has a deadly bite.

Hollow fangs pierce the skin and inject the venom.

{ Fig 1: Fang }

Eyes → ← Tongue

SNAKE SENSES

When a snake flicks out its forked tongue, it is actually smelling the air. The tongue collects scent molecules and then passes these to a sensor, called the Jacobson's organ, in the roof of the mouth.

FIERCE STRIKE

When a viper bites, it opens its mouth wide, and the long fangs flick forward before they are injected into its prey.

SEA SNAKE

Found in the warm waters of the Indian and Pacific oceans, sea snakes are some of the most venomous snakes on the planet. They spend most of their lives in the water, but still need to surface to breathe.

{ Fig 2: Banded sea snake }

SCARLET MACAW

Birds do not have teeth. They use their beaks to break up their food.

Backbone

THE scarlet macaw is a parrot that lives in the lush rain forests of South America. It feeds on nuts and seeds, which it crushes with its large beak. Parrots are very intelligent birds that are great at solving puzzles. They use twigs and leaves as tools to help them crack open nuts.

Breastbone

STANDING FIRM

Each foot has four toes. Two toes point forward and two point backward. This allows the bird to grip on to branches.

COLOR VISION

Birds can see a color called ultraviolet that we can't see. Scarlet macaws look spectacular to us with their red and blue feathers, but they probably look even more colorful to one another!

Keeping in Touch

Macaws fly together in pairs but sometimes come together in larger family groups. They keep in contact with others in their group by making loud screeching calls that can be heard several miles away.

Humerus

The scarlet macaw measures 30 inches from its head to the tips of its tail feathers.

Tailbone

Short finger bones have tiny wings, called alulae, attached to them.

A bird's wing has arm and finger bones. The main flight feathers, called primaries, are attached to the arm bones and the long finger bone.

Long finger bone

FLYING BIRDS

THE wings of flying birds come in many shapes and sizes. Some birds have long wings for gliding, while others have short wings that they flap many times a second.

Buzzard

HOVERING

This fawn-breasted hummingbird is using its fine flight control to hover in front of a flower and drink its sweet nectar.

{ Fig 1: Flight feathers }

Birds rotate their feathers to different angles during flight to give them maximum lift.

FLIGHT CONTROL

Hummingbirds are the masters of flight control. They can fly forward or backward, or they can hover in the same place. They have small wings that they flap between 20 and 100 times every second!

Tail feathers help the bird to steer.

HOLLOW BONES

A flying bird's bones are hollow. They are strong, but light enough for the bird to fly.

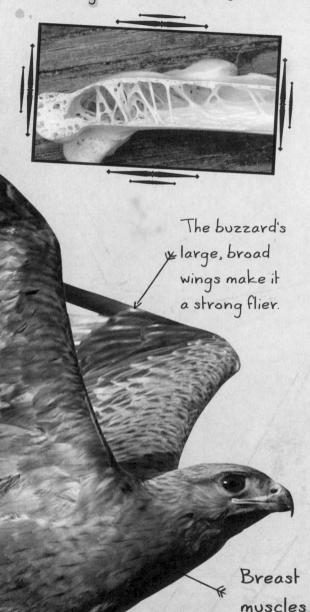

The buzzard's large, broad wings make it a strong flier.

Breast muscles

STRONG MUSCLES

A bird's largest muscles are its breast muscles. These provide the power for the downstroke of the wings. This produces a force, called lift, that keeps the bird in the air.

Cool Beaks

This toucan's beak is almost half the length of its body. The huge beak has a large surface area, which keeps the bird cool. It is filled with a very light, spongy substance.

{ Fig 2: Clark's grebes }

STAYING TOGETHER

Many birds stay with the same mate for their whole lives. They keep their partnerships strong using special greetings and dances. To seal their partnership, grebes run across the water together with their long necks extended upward.

CAPE PENGUIN

Wings have flattened bones.

PENGUINS use their short wings like flippers and spend most of their lives in the water, where they feed on fish and krill. Penguins live only in the Southern Hemisphere. The Cape penguin lives around the coast of southern Africa.

Ribs

HEAVY BONES
Unlike the bones of flying birds, a penguin's bones are heavy. The extra weight helps them dive more easily.

Breastbone

Feet are used like a rudder for steering.

Cape penguins swim at an average speed of 4 mph, but can reach a top speed of 12 mph when hunting.

DEEP DIVER

The Cape penguin hunts small fish such as anchovies. It can hold its breath for five minutes at a time and dive to a depth of up to 300 feet. It may swim more than 60 miles on a single feeding trip.

Long beak

Cape penguins stand 2 feet tall. The largest species, the emperor penguin, is twice as tall.

← Wishbone

Finger bones

SLEEK SHAPE

Penguins have streamlined bodies. This means that their shape allows them to cut a path through the water as they swim.

Nesting

Penguins come to land to lay their eggs and raise their young. Cape penguins make their nests on rocky beaches. The female lays two eggs, then both the mother and father take turns looking after them.

FLIGHTLESS BIRDS

PENGUINS use their wings to swim. Other flightless birds, such as ostriches, have useless wings but can run at high speeds.

BIG BIRD

The ostrich is the largest bird in the world. It also lays the largest eggs, which weigh more than 2 pounds. Like other big flightless birds, such as the emu, the ostrich is a fast runner, reaching speeds of up to 40 mph.

Ground Feeder

The kiwi lives in the forests of New Zealand. Its tiny wings are hidden under hairlike feathers. It has a sensitive beak, which it uses to search the forest floor for insects and worms.

Short wings are too small to use for flying.

Muscular legs

TOBOGGANING

For these emperor penguins, sliding along the ice is sometimes much easier than walking.

34

SENSING DANGER

For many large predators, such as leopards and lions, an ostrich makes a tasty meal. But they are not easy to catch. Their heads are nearly 10 feet above the ground, which means they can spot danger from a long way away.

Large eyes give the bird excellent vision.

Long neck

PORPOISING

Penguins sometimes fly out of the water as they swim in a movement called porpoising. They may do this to confuse predators.

DEAD AS A DODO

The dodo was a flightless bird that lived on the island of Mauritius in the Indian Ocean. It died out soon after humans arrived on the island. The dodo's eggs were eaten by the dogs and cats that people brought with them.

{ Fig 1: Dodo }

PLATYPUS

NO other animal on earth looks quite like the platypus, with its flat, ducklike snout. It spends most of its day in the water foraging for food. It feeds on shrimp, insect larvae, and worms, which it digs out of the riverbed with its sensitive snout.

Legs stick out of the side of the body like a lizard's legs.

TOOTHLESS
Instead of teeth, adult platypuses have horny pads inside their mouths.

Eye socket

The snout is made of skin stretched over a framework of bone.

EYES SHUT
The platypus hunts in muddy water, where eyes are of little use. In fact, it keeps its eyes tightly shut when it dives. It finds its prey by sensing the electricity that runs through their bodies. It does this with special sense receptors in its snout.

PADDLING

Platypuses swim by paddling their front legs. They use their back legs and tail to steer.

The platypus is 2 feet long from its head to the end of its tail.

The platypus stores fat in its tail.

Poisonous spur

Flattened rib cage

Hungry Hunter

The platypus has a big appetite and hunts for about ten hours a day. It spends most of the rest of its time asleep in a burrow in the riverbank.

Webbed feet

MONOTREMES

FOUND in Australia and New Guinea, echidnas and platypuses are monotremes. They are the only mammals that lay eggs.

{ Fig 1: Protective spines }

Long snout acts as both a mouth and a nose.

DEFENSE MECHANISM

When threatened, the echidna curls up into a tight ball.

ECHIDNA

The echidna uses its snout to root out ants and termites. Like the platypus, its snout can sense electricity in the bodies of its prey. It grabs the insects with its long, sticky tongue.

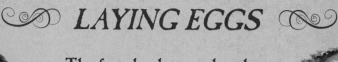

LAYING EGGS

The female platypus lays her eggs in a burrow. The young stay in the burrow for three to four months after they hatch, feeding on their mother's milk. When they are big enough, they emerge from the burrow for their first swim.

{ Fig 2: Platypus eggs }

{ Fig 3: Platypus young }

SPINES

The head, back, and tail of the echidna are covered in sharp spines, which protect it from predators. Baby echidnas, called puggles, are born without spines. The spines start to appear when they are about 50 days old.

Venomous Ankles

Male platypuses have venomous spurs on their rear ankles. They use these weapons in fights with other males.

WARM FUR

Platypuses are kept warm by their thick fur. The fur has two layers, which work together to trap air next to the skin. The air keeps the skin warm and dry, even when the platypus is diving.

RED KANGAROO

THE red kangaroo is a large marsupial that lives in the hot deserts of Australia. It has powerful back legs, which it uses to hop along at high speeds.

BACKBONE
The backbone is strong but flexible. It needs to bend to allow the kangaroo to hop.

Desert Traveler

Red kangaroos feed on grass and leaves. But there are few plants in the desert, so they must travel many miles a day to find enough to eat.

This large bone supports the mother's pouch and helps the animal to leap.

Neural spines

The tail has very strong bones. The kangaroo uses its tail to keep its balance as it hops.

Standing upright, a male red kangaroo is 7 feet tall, taller than an average man.

Eye socket

GREAT LEAPS

A red kangaroo can leap up to 30 feet in a single hop, and reach a top speed of more than 40 mph. It can also jump up to a height of 10 feet.

Short front legs

The shin bone is very long. Powerful leg muscles are attached to it.

DANGER

Red kangaroos have sharp claws and a powerful kick. No predators dare to take on an adult. However, dingoes and eagles will try to take its young.

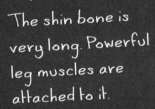

MARSUPIALS

MARSUPIALS are mammals that give birth to tiny young that grow inside a pouch in their mother's body.

SAFE PLACE

Kangaroo joeys stick their heads out of the pouch for weeks before they feel it is safe to leave.

{ Fig 1: Eastern quoll }

NIGHT HUNTER

Quolls spend the daytime tucked away in their dens, safe from predators. They come out to hunt at night, feeding on rabbits, small birds, and lizards. Quolls have keen senses, with large ears and sensitive noses to help them find prey in the dark.

BOXING MATCH

Male kangaroos fight one another in boxing matches. They stand on their hind legs and jab at their opponent. The one that stays upright wins.

Fighting kangaroos punch with their front legs.

Up a Gum Tree

The koala spends most of its life in eucalyptus trees, also called gum trees, feeding on the leaves. A baby koala clings to its mother's back as she moves around the tree.

JOEYS

A marsupial baby is called a joey. When it is born, a joey is the size of a bean, and is blind and furless. It crawls across its mother's fur to the pouch, where it feeds on its mother's milk. The joey stays in the pouch for up to a year.

The tail helps to support the body weight during a fight.

FIERCE DEVIL

The Tasmanian devil is a bad-tempered hunter. When it is excited, it makes a deafening screech.

43

FRUIT BAT

FRUIT BATS are the largest bats in the world. They have keen senses, which they use to track down their food of fruit, nectar, or pollen while swooping through the sky. When they find food, they fly up to the branches and grab on using sharp claws.

"THUMB"

The "thumb" of many bats sticks above the wing to form a claw, which they use to grasp and move about.

Forearm bones

"Finger" bones

The "fingers" of a bat are very long. Thin flaps of skin stretch between them to form the wings.

NIGHT VISION

Also known as the "flying fox," this type of bat is easy to spot because of its long, doglike snout. Inside this is a highly sensitive nose, which the bat uses to sniff out delicious fruit to chew or nectar-rich flowers to lick. Unlike other bats, flying foxes do not use echolocation to find their food and must rely on their heightened sense of smell.

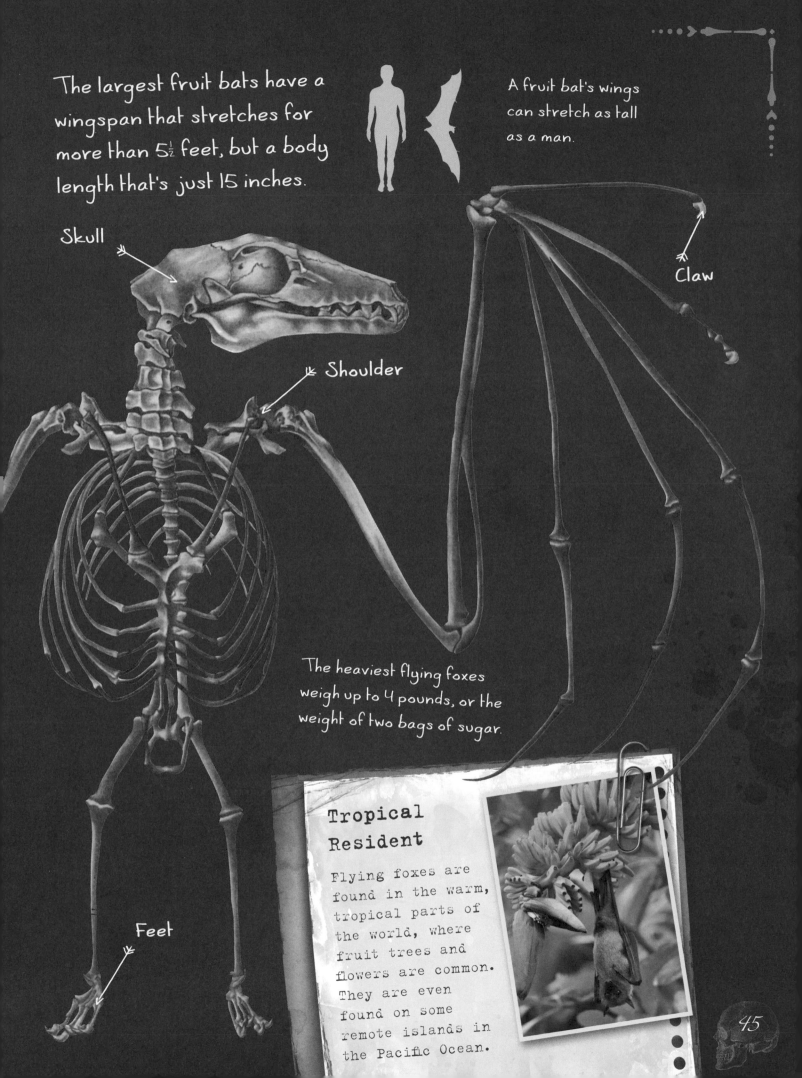

The largest fruit bats have a wingspan that stretches for more than 5½ feet, but a body length that's just 15 inches.

A fruit bat's wings can stretch as tall as a man.

Skull

Claw

Shoulder

The heaviest flying foxes weigh up to 4 pounds, or the weight of two bags of sugar.

Feet

Tropical Resident

Flying foxes are found in the warm, tropical parts of the world, where fruit trees and flowers are common. They are even found on some remote islands in the Pacific Ocean.

BATS

BATS are the only mammals capable of true flight, using their wings to flap through the air.

{ Fig 1: External ear }

While some bats use a keen sense of hearing, others have large eyes and rely on their sight.

FLYING HUNTER

While flying foxes like to eat fruits and flowers, many bats actively hunt for prey. They are so well suited to hunting in the dark that they can catch insects in midair and feed without having to land. Other bats feed in a more sinister way. Vampire bats land on large mammals, bite through their skin, and drink their blood!

THE WINGS

A bat's wings are so thin that the blood vessels running through them are clearly visible.

The long "fingers" stretch out to form the wings.

Bats that use echolocation have large ears to collect the echoes.

Large ears

SHARP TEETH
Some bats have very sharp teeth to eat insects, which they catch in midair.

Hearing Things

Many bats have a very keen sense of hearing and use sound to detect prey and what is around them. This is called echolocation. They produce a series of high-pitched clicks (so high that humans can't hear them) and listen for echoes made as these clicks bounce off objects or nearby prey.

PIPISTRELLE
These are some of the smallest bats, with a body length of just 1½ inches.

FLYING SQUIRRELS

Another mammal that takes to the air is the flying squirrel. It has flaps of skin that stretch between its legs, and it holds these out as wings. However, it is not capable of true flight and uses these wings to glide from tree to tree in its forest home.

{ Fig 2: Before takeoff }

{ Fig 3: In flight }

BEAVER

THE beaver is a rodent that spends most of its time in the water. Beavers are very hard workers. They cut down trees and use the branches to build their homes.

FELLING TREES

Beavers can fell trees with trunks up to 3 feet in diameter. They gnaw away at the trunk with their chisel-like front teeth.

BIG LUNGS
A beaver can stay underwater for up to 15 minutes at a time.

Knee

Dam Builder

Beavers build dams across shallow streams using a mixture of branches and mud. The dam creates a still pond behind it.

WARNING SIGNAL
When they sense danger, beavers signal to one another by slapping the water with their flat tails.

Webbed back feet

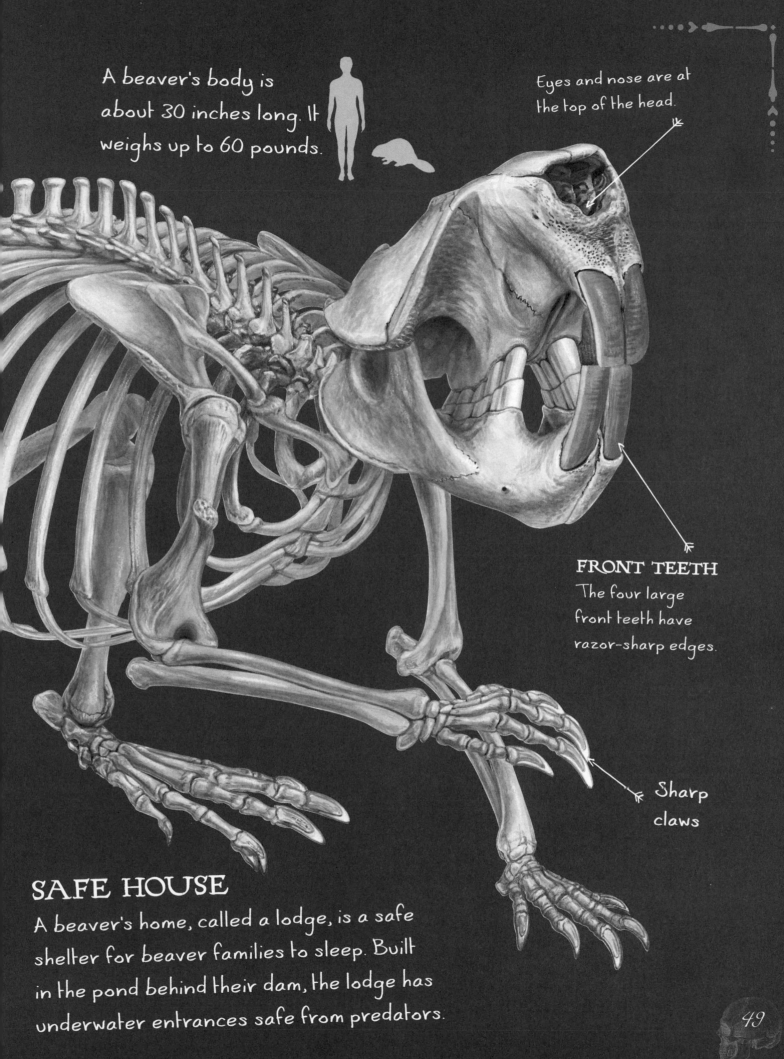

A beaver's body is about 30 inches long. It weighs up to 60 pounds.

Eyes and nose are at the top of the head.

FRONT TEETH
The four large front teeth have razor-sharp edges.

Sharp claws

SAFE HOUSE
A beaver's home, called a lodge, is a safe shelter for beaver families to sleep. Built in the pond behind their dam, the lodge has underwater entrances safe from predators.

RODENTS

RODENTS are mammals with a pair of strong front teeth that they use to chew through tough food.

Ears

Eye

Eyes, nose, and ears are at the top of the head, which makes swimming easier.

TREE CLIMBER

The Indian palm squirrel is an expert climber. It feeds on the nuts and fruits of the trees it climbs.

A young capybara sticks close to its mother.

CAPYBARA

Weighing as much as 100 pounds, the capybara is the largest rodent in the world. It lives in big family groups in swamps in South America, feeding mostly on grasses.

NAKED MOLE RAT

{ Fig 1: Naked mole rat }

Naked mole rats spend their whole lives underground. They dig tunnels with their front teeth and feed on the roots of plants. The rats live in large colonies of up to 200 animals, which all share the same network of tunnels.

DESERT RAT

The kangaroo rat lives in deserts. It takes shelter in a burrow during the day. At night, it comes out to feed on seeds, which it stores in special pouches in its cheeks.

The heartbeat slows to save energy as the dormouse sleeps.

BIG TEETH

The teeth at the front of a rodent's jaw keep growing throughout its life. This means that the teeth never wear out. The animals gnaw at wood or other hard surfaces to stop the teeth from growing too long.

Sleepy Mouse

Dormice survive the winter by hibernating. They may sleep for more than six months in a cold year, waking up occasionally to eat from a store of food that they have stashed nearby.

LION

The backbone is very flexible, which allows the lion to crouch as it hunts.

THE mighty lion is a big cat. It lives in family groups called prides. Lions hunt large prey such as zebra and wildebeest. They mostly hunt under cover of darkness and rest during the day.

Rib cage

MOTHER AND CUBS

Female lions, called lionesses, care for their cubs and teach them to hunt.

TAIL
The lion swings its tail from side to side as it runs. This helps it to keep its balance.

Knee

CLAWS
The claws fold backward when they are not needed. This keeps them sharp.

A fully grown lion is about 6 feet long and weighs as much as three men.

TEETH AND CLAWS

A lion's main weapons are its sharp claws and daggerlike canine teeth. It kills prey by sinking its teeth into its victim's neck.

Large muscles give the jaw a powerful bite.

Canine teeth

Pride Leaders

Most prides are ruled by large adult males. They have to fight rival males to keep control of their pride.

SCARY MANES

Male lions are slightly larger than the females. The males have a thick mane of hair around their necks, which makes them look even bigger and more scary.

CATS

WHETHER they are big or small, cats all look very similar. They are hunters that catch their prey using sharp teeth and claws.

HIDDEN DANGER

A tiger's stripes break up its shape, making it harder for prey to see it coming.

Tail

ROAR OR PURR?

Big cats, such as lions and tigers, make a blood-chilling roar. Small cats, such as pet cats, cannot roar, and meow or growl instead. But they can purr continuously, which big cats cannot do.

{ Fig 1: Striped fur }

Hind legs

BUILT FOR SPEED

The cheetah can run faster than any other land animal, reaching speeds of more than 60 mph. But it can only sprint over short distances, and its prey often escapes.

Cheetahs often live alone, but here two brothers have teamed up to hunt.

A Siberian tiger can cover 30 feet in a single leap.

The caracal is a little larger than a domestic cat. Its large ears give it excellent hearing. There are long tufts on the ends of its ears, which it twitches to communicate with other caracals.

{ Fig 2: Caracal }

MOUNTAIN TIGER

The largest big cat of all is the Siberian tiger, which can grow to be more than 10 feet long. It lives in the icy mountains of eastern Russia, where it hunts deer and wild boar.

BLACK PANTHER

Jaguars live in the forests of South and Central America. Most are orange with black spots, but some have bodies that are almost completely black.

Danger from Above

The leopard spends a lot of its time in trees. When it makes a kill, it drags the body up a tree to store it safely to eat at its leisure. Its spots hide it among the leaves, and it will sometimes leap on unsuspecting prey from above.

ELEPHANT SEAL

THE southern elephant seal is the largest of all seals. It lives in the icy waters of the Antarctic Ocean. A thick layer of fatty blubber under its skin protects it from the extreme cold.

DEEP-SEA DIVER

Elephant seals dive up to 1,000 feet down in search of fish. At these depths, water presses hard on their bodies. Bendy cartilage in their ribs stops their chests from breaking under the pressure.

Tibia and fibula

TOE BONES
The back feet have long toe bones, which the seal uses to push forward as it swims.

The leg bones are very short and are mostly contained in the seal's body.

Bull Seal

Male seals, called bulls, are twice the size of the females. They fight one another in bloody battles for the right to mate.

Females, called cows, give birth to a single pup.

Heavy skull

Sharp canine teeth

SWIMMER

Seals are clumsy on land, but they are very skilled swimmers. Their strong, flexible backs allow them to move easily through the water.

The bottom parts of the ribs are made from cartilage.

On land, the seal props itself up on its front flippers.

A male elephant seal is about 15 feet long and can weigh more than 6,000 pounds.

SEALS

WITH bodies shaped like torpedos and flippers for feet, these mammals are well suited to life in the water. They are found all over the world, but most prefer the colder waters far from the equator.

Short fur

Sea lions have visible external ear parts.

SEA LION

Unlike earless seals, which walk using only their front legs, sea lions can walk on all four legs. Their bodies are covered in thick, short fur.

HIDDEN ON THE ICE

Harp seal pups are born with white fur. This hides them from predators when their mothers leave them alone on the ice.

EARLESS SEALS

So-called earless seals, such as the elephant seal and the common seal, can still hear. But their ears do not have external flaps. This makes their bodies even more streamlined, allowing them to swim at greater speeds.

Beach Colony

Once a year, these Cape fur seals gather together on a beach to breed. The females give birth, then a few days later they mate with the males.

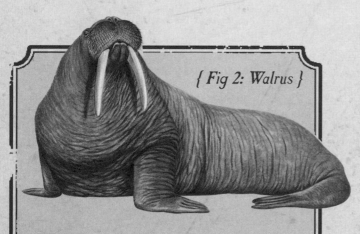

{ Fig 2: Walrus }

WALRUS

The walrus is a large animal that lives in the Arctic Ocean. It has two ivory tusks, which can be up to 3 feet long. The walrus digs out holes in the sea ice with its tusks. This allows it to swim under the ice and still have somewhere to breathe. Sensitive whiskers around its mouth help it to find clams, crabs, and other food in the murky water on the ocean floor.

UNDER THE ICE

The Weddell seal spends most of its life under the sea ice of Antarctica.

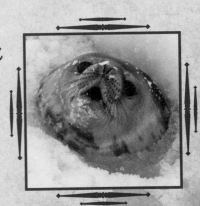

OCEAN HUNTER

The leopard seal is a fearsome hunter. It preys on smaller seals, penguins, and fish.

BLUE WHALE

THE blue whale is the largest animal that has ever lived on earth. Its heart alone is the size of a small car. This enormous animal feeds on tiny krill just a few inches long, but it can eat several million of them in a single meal.

LIGHTWEIGHT

As it is supported by the water, a whale's skeleton is fairly lightweight for its size.

HIP BONES

The tiny hip bones are not attached to the rest of the skeleton.

Backbone

DEEP BREATH

A blue whale's lungs can hold 1,300 gallons of air at a time. This allows the whale to hold its breath for more than 30 minutes when it dives.

TAIL BONES

A whale pushes itself through the water by swishing its tail up and down. Large muscles are attached to the spines on the tail bones.

The tail comes above the water as the whale starts a dive.

Shoulder blade

The neck is short to keep the body streamlined.

An adult blue whale is about 100 feet long and weighs 170 tons.

The jaw bones are long and curved.

The front flippers are each made up of five "fingers."

ARCTIC FEEDER

The blue whale spends much of the year in the Arctic or Antarctic oceans, where there are plenty of krill to eat. It moves to warmer waters to give birth.

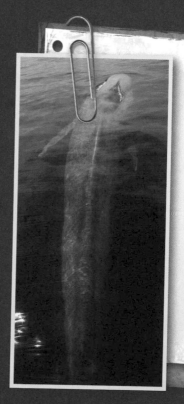

Protected

Before humans started to hunt them, there were hundreds of thousands of blue whales. Today, only about 10,000 are left. But they are now protected by law, and are no longer hunted.

WHALES AND DOLPHINS

WHALES and dolphins are mammals that spend their whole lives in the water. Some have teeth, while others have baleen plates.

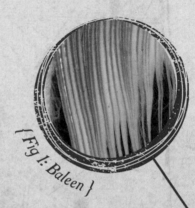

Baleen are thick, hairy plates in baleen whales' mouths.

{ Fig 1: Baleen }

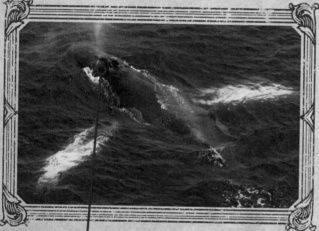

WHALE SONG
The humpback whale sings songs that can be heard by other whales hundreds of miles away.

A whale's nostrils, called blowholes, are at the top of its head.

Eye ⟩

{ Fig 2: Blowholes }

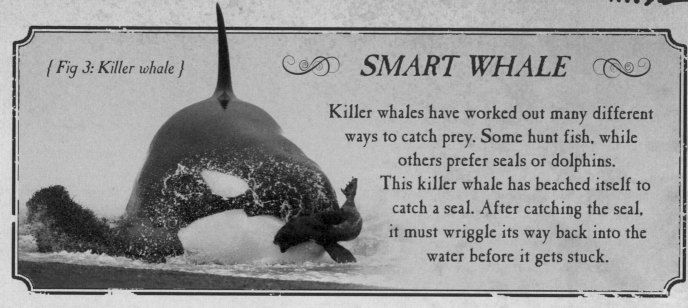

{ Fig 3: Killer whale }

SMART WHALE

Killer whales have worked out many different ways to catch prey. Some hunt fish, while others prefer seals or dolphins. This killer whale has beached itself to catch a seal. After catching the seal, it must wriggle its way back into the water before it gets stuck.

FILTER FEEDERS

Baleen whales, such as the blue whale and the gray whale, feed by filtering creatures from the water. They fill their mouths with water, then squeeze it out through their baleen plates. Any fish or krill in the water are caught in the baleen.

ACROBATIC DOLPHINS

Common dolphins are a little bigger than humans. They can swim at up to 40 mph and leap high out of the water.

← Jaw

OCEAN TRAVELER

Each year, gray whales swim from the Arctic Ocean to the coast of Mexico and back to the Arctic—a round trip of 12,000 miles.

Deep-Sea Hunter

The sperm whale dives to depths of up to two miles in search of its favorite meal—giant squid. Many of the whales have scars on their bodies from battles with squid.

AFRICAN ELEPHANT

BACKBONE
The backbone is thick and stiff. Elephants cannot bend over, but must kneel down or reach with their trunks.

ELEPHANTS are the biggest land animals in the world. The African elephant lives in grasslands and forests. It feeds on leaves, twigs, bark, fruit, and roots.

BIG APPETITE
An adult elephant needs to eat 400 pounds of food every day. That's the same weight as 1,000 apples!

Hip bone

TALKING FEET
Elephants sense vibrations in the ground with their feet, allowing them to "talk" over great distances. The rumble of their "voices" travels down their legs and through the ground.

A male African elephant may be over 10 feet tall and weigh more than 5 tons.

The skull is thick and strong to support the weight of the tusks and trunk.

Back teeth are 12 inches across.

Tusks are long front teeth. They may be up to 6 feet long.

Leg bones are very thick to support the heavy body.

Five toes on each foot

Sensitive Trunk

An elephant's trunk is made from its nose and upper lip. The trunk is strong but very sensitive. It can rip branches from a tree or gently stroke a newborn baby.

ELEPHANTS

FOUND in Africa and Asia, elephants are among the most intelligent animals in the world. They roam the forests and grasslands in close-knit family groups.

HEAD OF THE FAMILY

Each family group is led by an old female, known as the matriarch. Her experience is vital, as she knows where the best places to eat and drink are to be found.

PLAYING

Elephants enjoy one another's company. Youngsters are often at play, especially when they're in the water.

 **WOOLLY MAMMOTH**

The woolly mammoth was a large elephant-like creature that lived on the cold northern plains during the last ice age. It died out about 10,000 years ago.

{ Fig 1: Woolly mammoth }

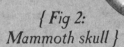

{ Fig 2: Mammoth skull }

Asian Elephants

Asian elephants are slightly smaller than their African cousins and have much smaller ears. Only males have long tusks.

LEAVING HOME

Female elephants stay with their family group their entire lives. Males leave the group when they grow up to live alone or with other males.

{ Fig 4: Tusk }

Elephants use their tusks to knock down trees and to dig.

The trunk is controlled by 60,000 muscles.

BIG BABY

A newborn baby elephant weighs more than a man.

Large ears help the elephant to lose heat and keep cool.

{ Fig 3: Nostrils }

The nostrils at the end of the trunk have an excellent sense of smell.

MOOSE

ALSO called the elk, the moose is the largest member of the deer family. It lives in northern forests, where it feeds on shoots and bark.

STAY AWAY

Moose are big and powerful and scare off most predators. An adult moose can kill a bear or wolf that tries to attack it.

Test of Strength

Male moose fight one another in tests of strength, called rutting. They push at one another's antlers until the weaker animal gives way.

BONY ANTLERS

Only male moose have antlers. The antlers start to grow in spring and are full-size by the mating season in the fall. They then drop off in winter.

Short tailbone

Knee

MIDDLE TOES

The moose walks on hooves formed by its two large middle toes.

Outside toe

NEURAL SPINES

The neural spines are spikes that stick up from the backbone. Powerful muscles stretch from the neural spines to the back of the skull. The muscles support the weight of the heavy head.

Antlers grow out of the top of the skull. They grow very quickly—by about half an inch a day.

Shoulder bone

CALF

The female gives birth in spring. Her calf will stay with her until the following spring, when she chases it away.

Radius

A male moose stands 6 feet high at the shoulder and weighs 1,500 pounds—as much as ten men.

DEER AND ANTELOPE

DEER and antelope are mammals that walk on the ends of their middle toes. Deer mostly live in cool areas. Most antelope are found on the hot African grasslands.

Long ears

As it feeds, a gerenuk's big ears listen for the rustling of any predators in the bushes.

{ Fig 1: Gerenuk head }

Long neck

GERENUK
This long-necked antelope lives in east Africa.

ON THE MOVE
Reindeer travel up to 3,000 miles each year in search of new pastures. They are strong swimmers and cross wide rivers and lakes on their journey.

Flexible hip joint allows the gerenuk to stand upright and reach high branches.

FANGED DEER

Male tufted deer have large tusklike incisor teeth. They use these fangs to fight off rivals.

Surviving Winter

During the long, cold winter, red deer survive by digging through the snow to eat the grass underneath. They also eat tree bark when snow covers the ground.

WATCHING OUT

To a lion, a leopard, or a hyena, an antelope is a prized catch, so antelopes must keep a constant lookout for predators. Their eyes are positioned on the sides of their heads, which allows them to see to the side as well as to the front.

INSECT PICKER

The oxpecker is a welcome friend to this impala. The bird picks itchy insects from the impala's fur.

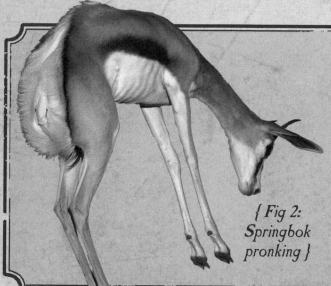

{ Fig 2: Springbok pronking }

✖ PRONKER ✖

When they sense danger, springboks leap into the air—an action called pronking. They jump as high as they can, reaching up to 13 feet off the ground. The high leaps show potential predators that the springboks are fit and strong, and that the predators had better look elsewhere for their next meal.

HORSE

HORSES are large grass-eating mammals. Most horses are domestic animals, which means that they live with humans. We use horses to pull farm machinery, for transportation, and for sport.

Neural spines

TAIL
The horse swishes its tail using muscles attached to spines at the top of the tail.

Knee socket

Hock

WILD HORSE
The only truly wild horse left in the world is the Przewalski's horse, which lives in Central Asia.

Fetlock

Measured to the tops of their shoulders, horses are 5 to 6 feet tall.

First thoracic vertebra

Eye socket

Nose bone

Long jaws contain rows of molar teeth for chewing grass.

A wide rib cage protects large lungs.

Herd Animals

Horses live together in herds. Each herd has a herd leader that decides what the herd should do.

LIGHT FEET

Horses have just one long toe on each foot. At the tip of each toe is a bone called the coffin bone, which is protected by the horny hoof. A horse's feet are narrow and light, which allows it to pick its legs up very quickly and gallop at high speed.

At the end of each toe is a tough hoof.

HORSES, ZEBRAS, AND DONKEYS

ZEBRAS are wild animals that live on the plains and mountains of Africa. Horses and donkeys are mostly domestic animals that live and work with humans.

BORN TO RUN

Horses and zebras run using a movement called a gallop. Racehorses can keep up a gallop of over 40 mph for more than half a mile.

Galloping horses

Kicking Out

When they are cornered, zebras and horses have a powerful weapon. They rear up on their front legs and kick out at an attacker with their hind legs.

MOOR PONIES

Ponies are small horses. These Dartmoor ponies need to be very hardy to survive on the wet and windy moorland.

BEAST OF BURDEN

A mule is the offspring of a male donkey and a female horse. It is faster than a donkey but can work longer hours than a horse. Mules are used in mountainous parts of the world to carry cargo across rough terrain.

{ Fig 1: Mules }

BRAYING DONKEYS

Donkeys make a loud braying noise. Their big ears can hear the brays of other donkeys up to two miles away.

Horses' hooves are often fitted with metal shoes to give them extra protection.

{ Fig 2: Hoof }

THREE-TOED SLOTH

At the end of each toe is a hook-shaped claw about 3 inches long.

Three-toed feet

YOU could easily walk right under a sloth without seeing it. A sloth spends most of its time motionless, hanging upside down from a tree and blending in with the leaves.

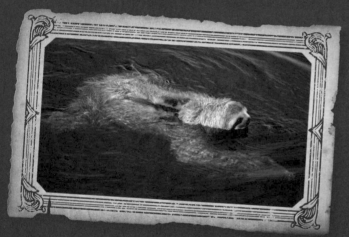

SWIMMING

Sloths are good swimmers. Sometimes they drop straight into a river from the trees to swim to a new location.

NIGHT FEEDER

Sloths eat and sleep in the trees. They rest during the day and feed at night. They come down to the ground about once a week to poop.

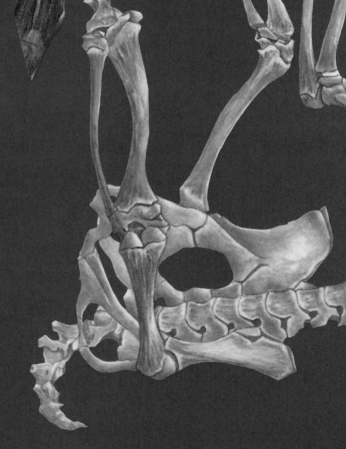

Green Camouflage

A sloth's brown fur has a green tinge to it. This is caused by algae growing in the fur. The green color helps to hide the animal from predators such as eagles.

LONG ARMS

The sloth pulls itself from branch to branch using its long front legs.

Shoulder bone

LONG NECK

There are nine bones in the neck. It is long and flexible, which allows the sloth to look down at the ground while it hangs.

Teeth are worn down by years of chewing tough leaves.

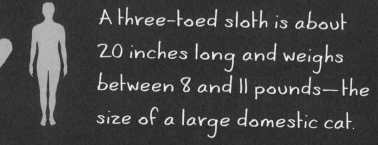

A three-toed sloth is about 20 inches long and weighs between 8 and 11 pounds—the size of a large domestic cat.

TREE MAMMALS

THE dense rain forests of South America are home to many different mammals. Monkeys swing acrobatically through the canopy. Sloths, on the other hand, keep as still as they can.

USEFUL TAIL
Amazonian monkeys use their tails to grip on to branches.

HOWLERS
Howler monkeys call to one another from the treetops. Their piercing howls can be clearly heard up to 3 miles away.

FOREST MONKEYS
More than 100 different species of monkey make their home in the Amazon rain forest. They have long tails that they use as an extra limb to swing from branch to branch.

The tail has a hairless tip that is grooved to get a good grip.

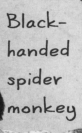

Black-handed spider monkey

BELLY CRAWL

The sloth's long arms and hooked claws are perfect for hanging from branches, but very bad for walking. When it comes down to the ground, it has to drag itself along with its claws. It returns to the safety of the trees as soon as it can.

{ Fig 1: Three-toed sloth }

Hang on Tight

Baby sloths cling to their mothers for the first nine months of their lives. When the baby grows up, its mother leaves it alone and finds herself a new territory.

TWO-TOED SLOTH

The two-toed sloth is slightly larger and more energetic than its three-toed relative.

Strong hands

SLOW DIGESTION

Sloths feed mostly on thick leaves. A sloth needs long periods of sleep and rest in between feeding so that it can digest its tough diet.

SLOTH FEEDING

A sloth holds a branch still with its claws as it munches on the leaves.

79

GIANT ANTEATER

'THIS large mammal lives on a diet of ants and termites. It tears open an ants' nest with its claws, then flicks out its tongue. The tongue is covered in tiny spines, which catch the ants.

There is a small hump at the back of the neck. The neck is thicker than the head.

HYOID BONES

The tongue is moved by the hyoid bones. Muscles attached to the hyoid can flick the tongue in and out of the mouth up to three times a second.

Long snout

Broad ribs

The anteater walks on its front knuckles, with its long claws curled up.

BUSHY TAIL

The anteater's body is covered in long hairs. When it sleeps, it uses its bushy tail like a blanket, covering its body to keep warm.

From nose to tail, a giant anteater is about 6 feet long. Its head is about 12 inches long.

Special joints give the backbone extra strength.

NEST RAIDER

A giant anteater will dig up about 200 nests in a day. The ants and termites fight back with stinging bites, and the anteater is forced out after about a minute. This means that enough insects will survive for the colony to recover.

Tail

Thigh bone

TOOTHLESS

With tubelike jaws and no teeth, an anteater does not chew its food. It crushes insects against its palate before swallowing them whole.

Hidden Pup

Female anteaters carry their pups on their backs. The markings on the pup's fur line up with its mother's markings. This hides the pup from predators.

ANTEATERS

Large ears give a sharp sense of hearing.

FOUND only in North and South America, the slow-moving anteaters are closely related to sloths. They are shy animals, but will attack if backed into a corner.

DEFENSE POSE

When it feels threatened, the tamandua rears up on its hind legs so that it can attack with its front claws. It also gives off a foul-smelling gas to keep predators away.

Southern tamandua

DIGGER

The tamandua's forearms have strong muscles. It needs them to dig open ant and termite nests.

A giant anteater's tongue is more than 20 inches long—longer than its head.

SNIFFING AROUND

Anteaters have small eyes and poor eyesight. But their noses are around 40 times more sensitive than a human nose. They sniff their way to their meals.

CLAWS

The claws on the two middle fingers are long, curved digging tools. They also make fearsome weapons.

Silky Anteater

The silky anteater gets its name from the silk cotton trees in which it lives. It holds on to the tree's branch with its back legs and tail while it searches for insects with its front arms.

⌘ ARMADILLOS ⌘

With tough, leathery armor covering their backs and heads, armadillos are well protected against predators. They dig out deep burrows to sleep in during the day, coming out at night to hunt for insects.

{ Fig 2: Pink fairy armadillo }

{ Fig 3: Nine-banded armadillo }

GORILLA

GORILLAS are apes that live in the dense forests of central Africa. They are large and powerful, but spend most of their time feeding peacefully on plants.

MOUNTAIN GORILLAS

Some gorilla groups live high in the mountains. They have thicker fur to keep them warm in the cold conditions.

FAMILY GROUP

Gorillas live in small groups of about ten, with one large male and several females and their young. The male defends the group from attackers.

KNUCKLE WALKING

A gorilla usually walks on all fours, leaning on its knuckles. Its arms are longer than its legs, making walking on all fours easier.

Thigh bone

Legs are very straight, making walking upright difficult.

The big toe can touch all the other toes, allowing the gorilla to hold objects with its feet.

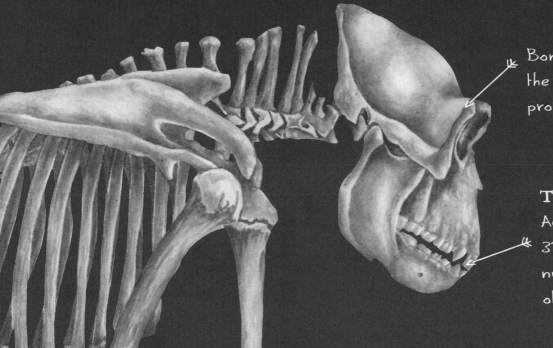

Bony ridge on the forehead protects the eyes.

TEETH
Adult gorillas have 32 teeth—the same number as all other apes.

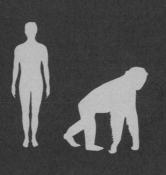

A male gorilla stands about 6 feet tall. This is the same height as a human, but a gorilla is much heavier—up to four times the weight.

Silverback

At about the age of 12, male gorillas grow silvery white hairs on their backs. When they are fully grown, the males will leave their group to start their own families.

Gorillas walk on their front knuckles.

APES

THE apes are a group of primates. They all have expressive faces, which they use to show one another how they are feeling.

Chimps and bonobos live in the forests of central Africa.

Bonobo infant

USING TOOLS

This chimpanzee is crushing nuts using a piece of wood as a tool.

Female bonobos form close bonds with their babies, which will last for their entire lives.

Bonobo mother

SOCIAL GROUPS

Chimpanzees and bonobos look very similar, but live in different kinds of social groups. Chimp groups are dominated by males, and order is kept by the threat of violence. In bonobo groups, the females dominate and there is less violent conflict.

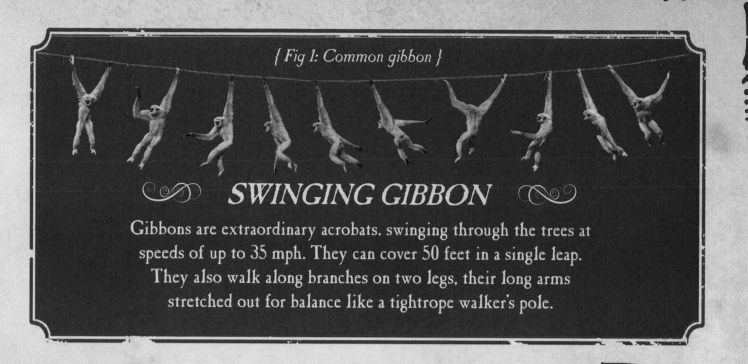

{ Fig 1: Common gibbon }

SWINGING GIBBON

Gibbons are extraordinary acrobats. swinging through the trees at speeds of up to 35 mph. They can cover 50 feet in a single leap. They also walk along branches on two legs, their long arms stretched out for balance like a tightrope walker's pole.

GREAT APES

Unlike monkeys, apes have no visible tails. There are two groups of apes. The great apes include orangutans, gorillas, bonobos, and chimps. The lesser apes, or gibbons, are smaller and more agile than the great apes.

Man of the Forest

Orangutans, whose name means "man of the forest," live in the rain forests of Borneo and Sumatra. They spend most of their time in the trees.

CHEST BEATER

When they are threatened. gorillas beat their chests with their fists and make a loud hooting sound to intimidate their opponents.

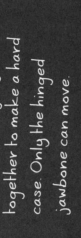

The rounded skull protects our large brains. The skull is made of 22 bones. Of these, 21 are fused tightly together to make a hard case. Only the hinged jawbone can move.

RIB CAGE
The rib cage is a framework of bones that protects our lungs and heart. As we breathe in, muscles pull at the rib cage to make it larger to make room for the lungs to fill with air.

Elbow

Bowl-shaped hip bones

HUMANS

HUMANS walk on two legs. This frees up our hands to explore the world. To help us make full use of our hands, we have developed big brains that let us think and solve problems.

ALL-AROUND ATHLETES
Humans can run, jump, swim, climb, and throw. Our all-around skills allow us to survive in many different kinds of habitats.

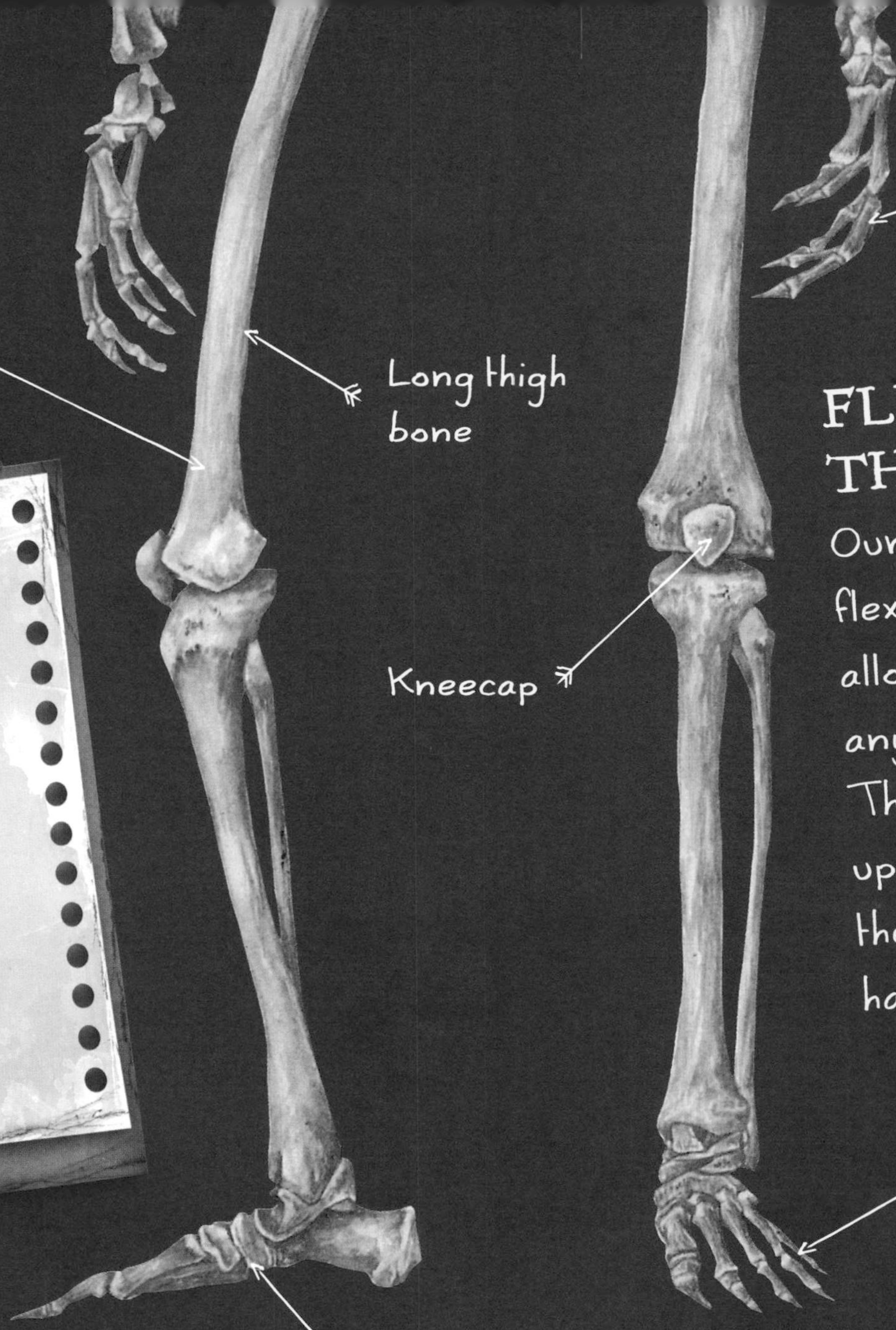

There are 27 bones in each hand.

FLEXIBLE THUMBS

Our thumbs have flexible joints that allow them to touch any of the fingers. This allows us to pick up objects and turn them around in our hands to examine them.

Flat feet with short toes provide a solid platform for walking.

Long thigh bone

Kneecap

There are 26 bones in each foot.

The thigh bones are angled to place the legs right under our bodies. This makes walking on two legs much easier.

Baby Bones

A newborn baby's skeleton is made of more than 300 bones. As the baby grows, some of these bones join together. An adult human skeleton has just 206 bones.

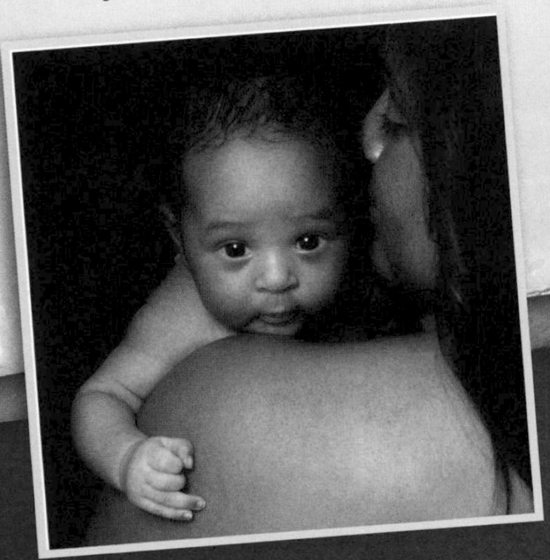

AMAZING SKELETON FACTS

BIGGEST BONE

The largest bone in the animal kingdom is the jawbone of the blue whale. It is up to 20 feet long and weighs about 1,300 pounds. That's as heavy as a small car.

Bone marrow

LONG NECK

A giraffe's neck is 6½ feet long. It is made up of seven bones. That's the same number of bones as there are in the human neck, but a giraffe's neck bones are much longer.

Each neck bone is nearly 12 inches long.

BLOOD FACTORY

Bones are hard and stiff, but they are also alive. Nerves and blood vessels run through them. At the center of many bones is a soft substance called bone marrow. One of the bone marrow's jobs is to make red blood cells. The bones in your body make two million new blood cells every second!

Blue whale jawbone

TUSKED WHALE

The narwhal has a single tusk that grows up to 10 feet long. The tusk is its left canine tooth. It is hollow and light, weighing about 22 pounds.

SHARK TEETH

A great white shark has about 300 razor-sharp teeth, arranged in up to seven rows. When a tooth falls out, another grows back in its place.

The tooth has a sawlike edge to rip flesh.

Actual size

Tail

BREAKING BONES

Lizards can deliberately break off part of their skeleton. They lose their tails to escape from the jaws of a predator. A new tail grows back in a few weeks.

EAR BONES

The smallest bones in the human body are three tiny bones in the ear called the hammer, the anvil, and the stirrup. These bones carry vibrations from the eardrum into the inner ear, where they are heard as sounds.

Actual size

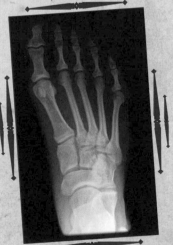

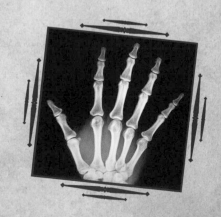

LONG THIGH

The longest bone in the human body is the thigh bone, or femur. It is almost one third of the length of the whole body.

FLOATING BONE

The only bone in the human body that is not joined to another bone at a joint is the hyoid bone in the throat.

FEET AND HANDS

More than half the bones in the human body are found in the feet and hands.

BONE NAMES

THIS lion's bones have been separated to show you all the main parts that make up an animal's skeleton.

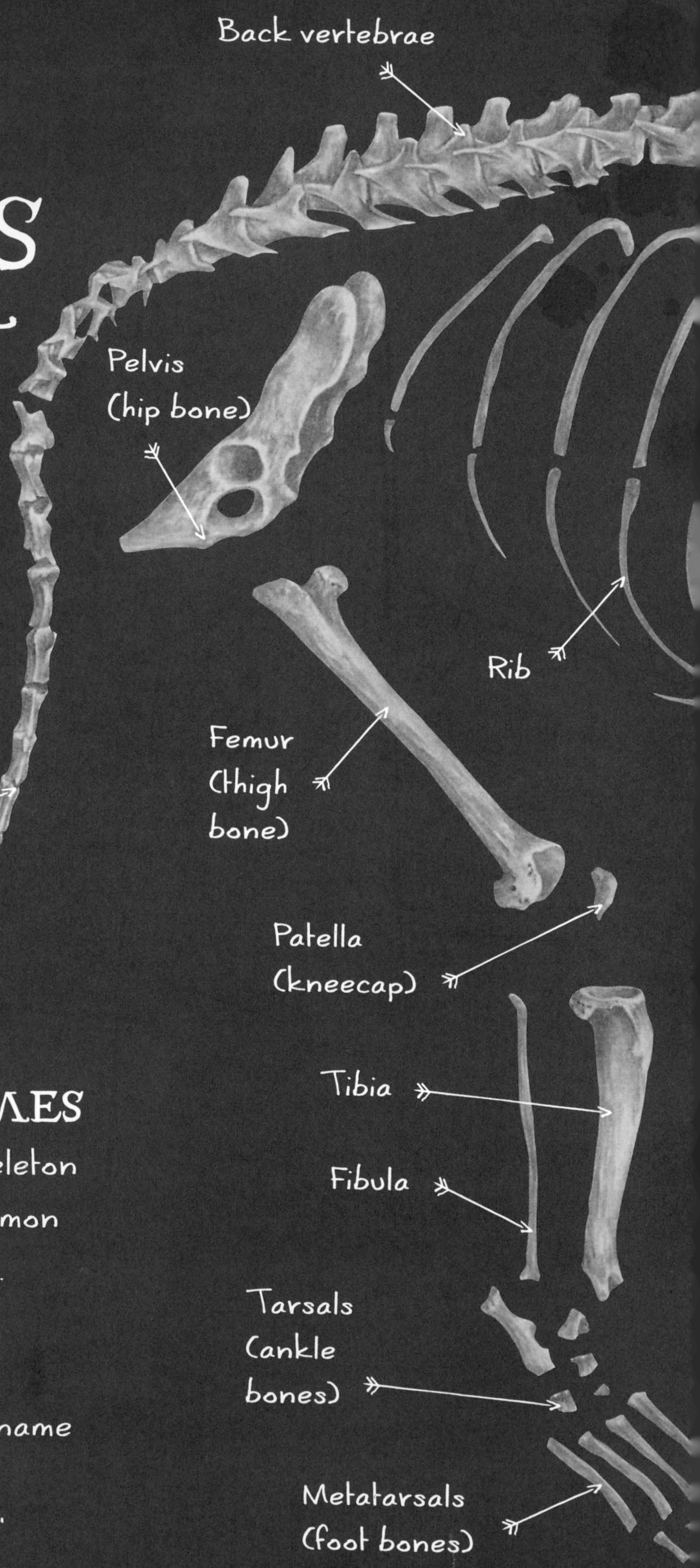

Tail vertebrae

SCIENTIFIC NAMES

Many of the bones in a skeleton have two names—their common name and a scientific name. The scientific name usually refers to the bone's shape. For instance, the scientific name for the kneecap is "patella," which is Latin for "little pan."

Back vertebrae

Pelvis (hip bone)

Rib

Femur (thigh bone)

Patella (kneecap)

Tibia

Fibula

Tarsals (ankle bones)

Metatarsals (foot bones)

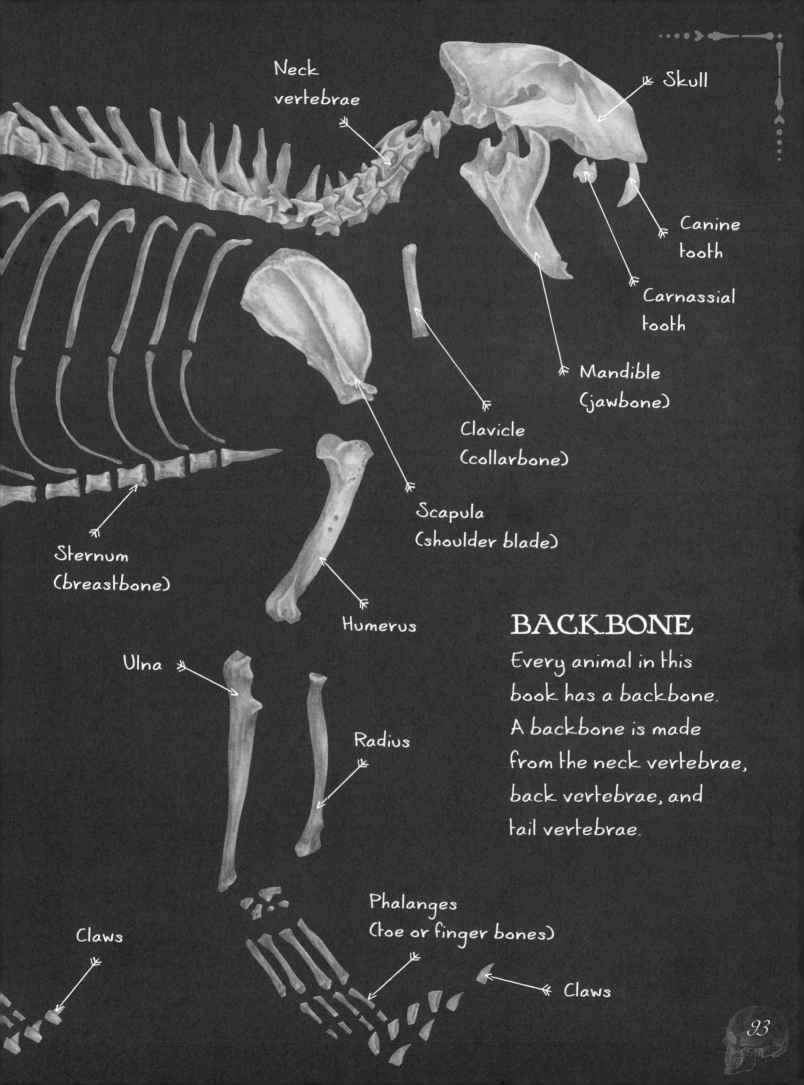

Neck vertebrae

Skull

Canine tooth

Carnassial tooth

Mandible (jawbone)

Clavicle (collarbone)

Scapula (shoulder blade)

Sternum (breastbone)

Humerus

Ulna

Radius

BACKBONE

Every animal in this book has a backbone. A backbone is made from the neck vertebrae, back vertebrae, and tail vertebrae.

Phalanges (toe or finger bones)

Claws

Claws

GLOSSARY

AMPHIBIAN
An animal that can live on land and in water. Many amphibians start their lives as larvae living in water, then emerge onto land as adults.

BALEEN
Plates made of keratin inside the mouths of some whales, such as humpback whales and blue whales. The whales use the baleen plates to filter small fish and krill from the water.

BEAK
The hard mouthparts of a bird and some other animals, such as turtles. Birds' beaks come in many shapes, depending on their diet. Also called a bill.

BIRD
An animal with feathers whose front limbs are wings. Birds lay eggs and are warm-blooded, meaning that they keep their temperature constant.

BLOWHOLE
A hole at the top of the heads of whales and dolphins. The animals only breathe through their blowholes, not through their mouths.

CARTILAGE
A flexible substance found at the joints of bones, in the rib cage, and in our ears and noses. A shark's whole skeleton is made of cartilage.

ECHOLOCATION
A system of sounds used by animals such as bats and dolphins to find prey and move around in the dark. Sounds bounce off an object and the animal judges the object's position by listening to the echo.

FINS
Flaps on the sides of sea creatures such as fish and whales that they use to swim.

FISH
Animals that live in water and breathe using gills. Fish use muscles attached to their backbones and their fins to move their bodies in an S shape.

FLIPPERS
Limbs of some sea-going animals that are used for swimming. In penguins, the wings have adapted to become flippers. In turtles and seals, the flippers are their modified arms and legs.

GILL
A body part in fish and some amphibians that allows them to breathe underwater. The gills take in oxygen that is dissolved in the water.

GLAND
A body part that makes chemicals to control processes such as growth. Some animals have glands that make poisons or smelly chemicals that they use to attack other animals.

HIBERNATE
To go into a deep sleeplike state to survive the cold of winter. When animals hibernate, their bodies cool and their heart rate slows down to save energy.

HOOF
The horny tip of the toes of some mammals, which they use to walk on. Sheep, deer, and pigs have two hooves on each foot. Horses and zebras have just one on each foot.

ICE AGE

A period when large parts of the planet are covered in snow and ice. There have been many ice ages in Earth's history. The last ice age ended about 10,000 years ago.

INVERTEBRATE

An animal that does not have a backbone. Most animals are invertebrates. Some, such as insects, have a hard outer exoskeleton. Others, such as worms and squid, have completely soft bodies.

KERATIN

A tough protein that our hair and nails are made from. The scales, horns, shells, and hooves of many animals are also made of keratin.

KRILL

Small shrimplike creatures that are found in large numbers in the oceans. They vary in size from $\frac{1}{2}$ inch to 6 inches long. Krill are the main food of many fish, squid, and whales.

LARVA

The young of animals such as fish, insects, and amphibians. The larvae look completely different from the adults, and often live in very different places. For example, the larvae of frogs, called tadpoles, live under water, while the adults live mostly on land.

MAMMALS

A group of warm-blooded animals that have hairy bodies. Female mammals produce milk from glands in their skin, which they use to feed their young.

MARSUPIALS

A group of mammals that give birth to very small young that the mothers carry in a pouch while they grow. Marsupials include kangaroos, koalas, and opossums.

MUSCLE

A body part that can contract or squeeze. Muscles are attached to bones and move them.

PRIMATES

A group of mammals that have large brains. Primates have hands or feet that can grasp and pick up objects. Monkeys, lemurs, and chimpanzees are all primates.

REPTILES

A group of animals that have scaly skin and lay eggs. Reptiles are cold-blooded, which means that they cannot keep their body temperature constant. Crocodiles, turtles, and lizards are all reptiles.

SCALES

Small protective plates that form part of the outer skin of some animals. Fish have bony scales, while reptiles and birds have scales made of keratin.

SOCIAL GROUP

A collection of animals of the same species, often closely related to one another, who work together to find food or shelter.

SPECIES

A kind of living thing. Members of the same species are very similar to one another and can breed and produce offspring.

TUSK

An enlarged tooth that sticks out of an animal's mouth. Elephants and walruses have two tusks in their upper jaws.

VERTEBRATE

An animal with a backbone. The backbone is a row of bones called vertebrae. Running through the vertebrae is a spinal cord, which is a bundle of nerves that carry messages between the brain and other parts of the body.

INDEX

alligator 22, 23
amphibians 12–15
anteater 80–83
antelope 70–71
antlers 68, 69
apes 84–87
armadillo 83
axolotl 15
backbone 6, 13, 40, 52, 64, 93
baleen 62, 63
bats 6, 7, 44–47
beak 17, 28, 31
beaver 48–49
birds 28–35
blowhole 62
blubber 56
bone marrow 90
bonobo 86
caecilian 15
camouflage 77
capybara 50
caracal 55
cartilage 11, 57
cats 52–55
cheetah 54
chimpanzee 86
cod 8–9
constrictor 26
crocodile 20–21
crocodilian 20–23
deer 70–71
dodo 35
dolphin 62, 63

domestication 72
donkey 74–75
dormouse 51
ears 59, 67, 91
echidna 38
echolocation 47
elephants 64–67
eyes 10, 36, 71
fangs 24, 27
fish 8–11
flight 30, 31, 46
flightless birds 34–35
flippers 7, 16, 57
flying fox 44, 46
flying squirrel 47
frogs 12–13, 14
gerenuk 70
gharial 22, 23
gibbon 87
gills 10, 11, 15
giraffe 90
gorilla 84–85, 87
hands 7, 88, 91
hearing 47
hibernation 13, 51
hoof 68, 73
horse 72–75
humans 7, 88–89, 91
hummingbird 30
intelligence 28, 66
jaguar 55
jaws 22, 24, 90
kangaroo 40–43
kiwi 34

knuckle walking 80, 84
koala 43
larvae 10, 15
legs 6, 40, 84, 89
leopard 55
lion 52, 53, 92–93
lizard 91
lungs 12, 19, 48, 60
macaw 28, 29
mammal 6, 38, 46, 62, 78, 79
marsupial 40–43
monkey 78
monotreme 36–39
moose 68, 69
mule 75
muscle 5, 22, 31, 60
narwhal 90
newt 14
orangutan 87
ostrich 34, 35
parrot 28–29
penguin 32–35
platypus 36–39
pony 74
pouch 40, 42, 43
quoll 42
rat 51
rattlesnake 26
reindeer 70
reptiles 19, 20
ribs 6, 25, 88
rodents 48–51
sailfish 10
salamander 14, 15
scales 22, 26
sea lion 58

sea snake 27
seal 6, 7, 56–59
shark 11, 91
shell 16, 19
sight 29, 44
skin 12, 14
skull 6, 65, 88
sloth 76–77, 79
snake 24–27
springbok 71
squirrel 50
swimming 57, 76
tadpole 15
tail 21, 40, 60, 78, 91
Tasmanian devil 43
thumb 44, 89
tiger 54–55
tongue 27, 38, 80, 83
tortoise 18
toucan 31
trunk 65, 67
turtle 16, 19
tusks 59, 65, 90
vampire bat 46
venom 24, 27, 39
vertebrae 25, 93
vertebrate 6, 7
viper 24, 25
viperfish 11
walrus 59
whale 60, 63, 90
wings 6, 7, 29, 30, 32, 45, 46
woolly mammoth 66
zebra 74